Moods of the
NORTHUMBERLAND COAST

TONY HOPKINS

HALSGROVE

First published in Great Britain in 2003
Reprinted 2007

British Library Cataloguing-in-Publication Data
A CIP record for this title is available from the British Library

ISBN 978 1 84114 309 5

HALSGROVE
Halsgrove House
Ryelands Farm Industrial Estate
Bagley Green, Wellington
Somerset TA21 9PZ
T: 01823 653777
F: 01823 665294
email: sales@halsgrove.com
website: www.halsgrove.com

Printed and bound by D'Auria Industrie Grafiche Spa, Italy

INTRODUCTION

Leaf through the pages of this book and the essential nature of the Northumberland coast will be apparent. It is a place of wide sandy bays, low rocky headlands, castles, islands, seabird colonies, gusty winds and bright sunshine. It is often deserted, sometimes wild and desolate, and always a joy to visit.

History is etched into every stone along the coast. The Lindisfarne Gospel and Bede's Ecclesiastical History were written on Holy Island. Saint Cuthbert spent years as a hermit on the Farne Islands and befriended the animals and birds, so much so that they are still the most approachable wild creatures in Britain. The Vikings made a big impact all along this coast, as did the Angles whose King Ida founded the Northumbrian kingdom from a stronghold at Bamburgh. Queen Mary fled to Bamburgh during the Wars of the Roses. John of Gaunt made a border fortress out of Dunstanburgh. Shakespeare set scenes in *Henry IV* at Warkworth Castle. And Grace Darling helped to save some shipwrecked sailors and became a Victorian heroine.

According to Daniel Defoe, Northumberland is 'a long coasting county'. In fact it stretches for 60 miles, from Seaton Sluice to Berwick upon Tweed. Most of it is designated an Area of Outstanding Natural Beauty and a Heritage Coast, recognising the coast's cultural and natural importance as well as the quality of its landscape.

Wide bays and dune ridges take up most of the space, along with shallow cliffs and carrs of Lower Carboniferous sandstone, shale and limestone. Into these buckled sediments were intruded magma which cooled into quartz dolerite: this hard dark grey rock now outcrops as ridges ('heughs') which form the classic promontories for castles and lighthouses, and the sea cliffs with nesting kittiwakes and fulmars. To the north and south there is millstone grit and coal measures, ensuring every mile of the 'coasting county' is complex and compelling.

Everyone responds differently to a place. This book is my own interpretation of a favourite stretch of coast, based on 20 years of photographing and writing about it. The choice of what to photograph, and the selection of which images to use and how to order them in this book, is arbitrary and personal. As it should be.

I prefer to work quickly: there is no point in waiting patiently for the right light when the tideline and clouds can change the composition in a few seconds. If I do have to wait I usually give up after an hour – there will always be another day. I only use a tripod for twilight shots and when a depth of field is essential; to frame a shot often means you are standing on tiptoe or lying flat on the ground, where a tripod would be impractical. I also do a lot of walking to get to locations and my tripod gets heavy when it is not used. On the other hand, to get good pictures of flowers, sunsets, waterfalls, there is no alternative. It helps to be flexible.

My field equipment usually consists of a rucksack stuffed with towels and bubble wrap, among which I nestle a Nikon (sometimes two) and three lenses – no cases. I rarely use my medium format camera these days, nor do I yet trust digital cameras. I never use filters, except a simple skylight to protect lenses.

Most of the pictures in this book were taken on Provia film, which seems to me to provide the best compromise between speed, grain and colour saturation. The only worthwhile trick I know in photography is to balance intuition with an organised technique – to develop an eye for an opportunity, the right angle, the right moment.

There are several peculiarities about the Northumberland coast that influence photography. The coastal zone is narrow – there are few big inlets or estuaries, and the change from sand-dunes to farmland is abrupt. A matter of a few steps and the sea might as well be a hundred miles away. Often, the weather changes abruptly too – it will be sunny on the beach or out to sea but dull and dreary inland. Clouds pirouette rather than scud across. Sea mists ('frets') can roll in like an express train and then hang around for days.

Finally, because this is the east coast, the best photographs are taken in the morning. This means that unlike a book of west coast pictures, where there might be a crimson / orange cast, much of this book is bathed in magenta.

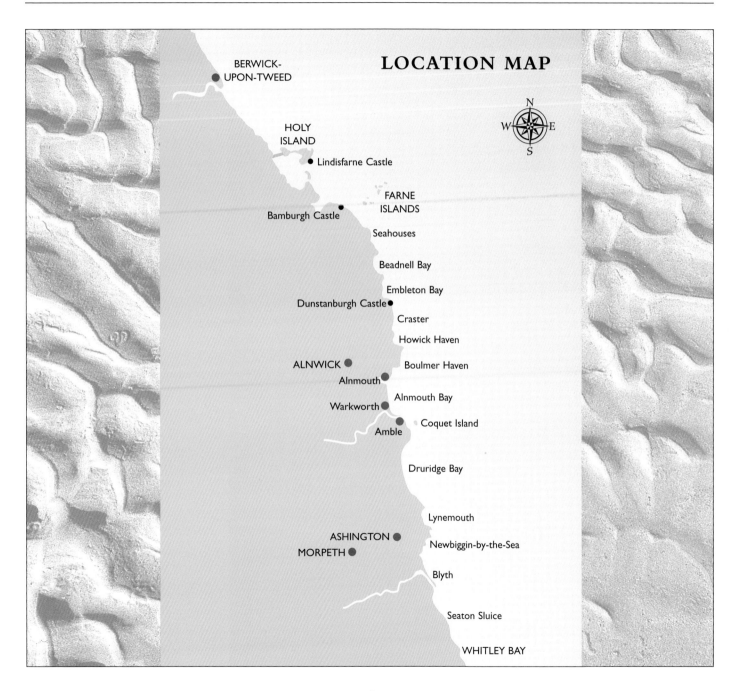

LOCATION MAP

BERWICK-
UPON-TWEED

HOLY
ISLAND

● Lindisfarne Castle

FARNE
ISLANDS

Bamburgh Castle

Seahouses

Beadnell Bay

Embleton Bay

Dunstanburgh Castle ●

Craster

Howick Haven

ALNWICK ●

Boulmer Haven

Alnmouth

Alnmouth Bay

Warkworth

Coquet Island

Amble

Druridge Bay

Lynemouth

ASHINGTON ●

Newbiggin-by-the-Sea

MORPETH ●

Blyth

Seaton Sluice

WHITLEY BAY

Sunrise over Bamburgh
Castle, from Beal Sands
on the causeway to
Holy Island.

Sailing boats in a south-westerly breeze north of Coquet Island.

Coquet Island lighthouse flashing in the early morning twilight, seen from the dune ridge of Amble Braid.

Half an hour later at Amble Braid: the sun has climbed above the cloud bank and bathed the sea and shore in golden sunshine. Half an hour later again and it was raining.

Coquet Island from
the water outfall at
Low Hauxley. Coquet
is managed as a wildlife
reserve and no-one
is allowed to land.
Nesting seabirds include
roseate terns and
eider ducks – this is
their most southerly
breeding colony.

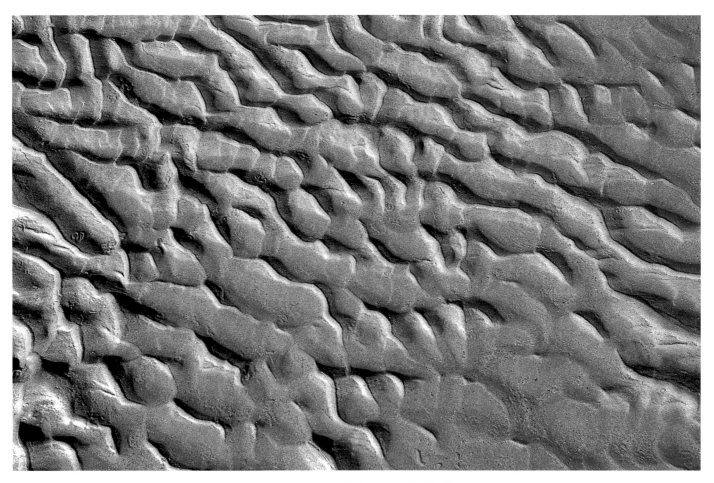

Ripple patterns on drying sand, Beadnell Bay.

An ebbing tide at Druridge Bay has exposed deep ripple patterns. A gusting north-west wind is catching the water surface between the sand ridges.

Sand patterns on the shore at Newton.

A calm and quiet morning at low tide. Looking north over Embleton Bay towards Newton Point.

Seawater channels around dolerite boulders on the south shore at Embleton. An hour after dawn and the sun is about to appear for the first time, over the back of a weather front on its way to the Low Countries.

Alnmouth Bay from the slopes of Castle Hill, on the opposite bank of the River Aln.
The harbour once exported grain and imported guano: a lucrative business in the nineteenth century.

Low tide at Alnmouth Bay and it is obvious why only small
boats can reach the moorings in the harbour to the west (left).

Midwinter at Alnmouth, looking south-west over marshland and the town's playing field.

A still day and a very low tide looking across the Aln estuary south over the dune ridge and Birling Carrs towards Amble.

A May morning at Cresswell, the village at the southern tip of Druridge Bay.

On the dune ridge at Cresswell. Marram grass and lyme grass (at the botton left of the picture) bind the sand and start the process of dune building and fixing.

South towards Snab Point, close to Lynemouth. Coal seams outcrop on the sea bed and underground:
this is a famous mining area and the beach is often covered in a tide-line of 'sea coal'.

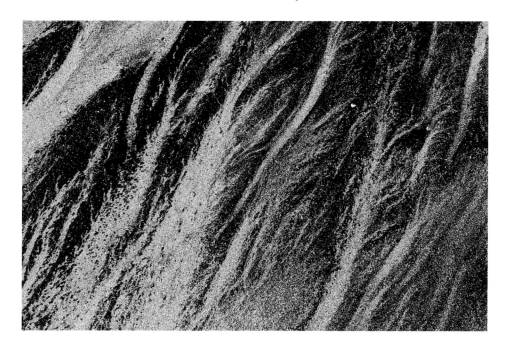

Fine grains of coal washing over sand on the Lynemouth beach.

Small coal pebbles, like jet beads, washed in on the tide at Lynemouth.

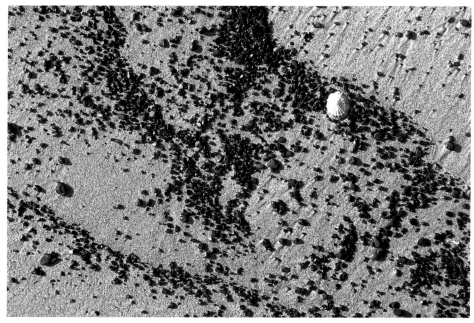

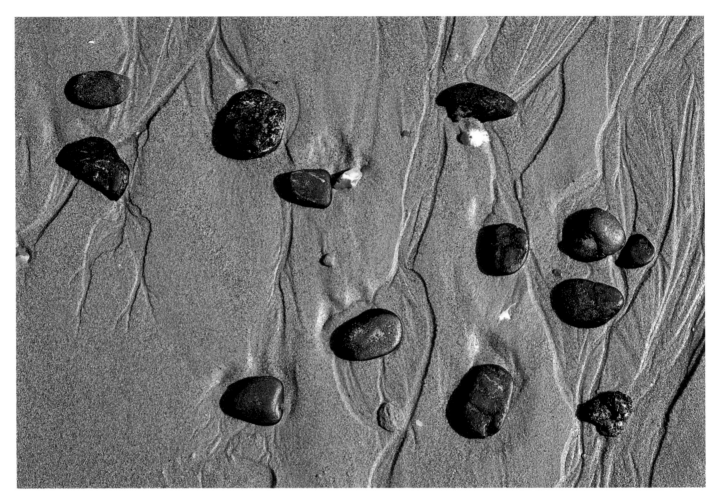

Coal pebbles on the beach at Amble. People in Northumberland gather sea coal as free fuel,
but it burns badly and gives off a lot of smoke and sulphur.

Firm sand is excellent for leaving tell-tale tracks of wildlife. These footprints are of a mink: in Northumberland both otters and mink are usually associated with rivers rather than the sea.

Sunlight bouncing off a fog bank over the North Sea on a March morning.
Dunstanburgh Castle has just appeared as early mist has burnt off.

Dunstanburgh Castle from the south: high tide and a busy sea. The castle was a Lancastrian stronghold in the Wars of the Roses, but has been a ruin for centuries.

Druridge Bay, close to Druridge village and Widdrington. The great sweep of
the bay is a popular local attraction, though you can often have it to yourself.

Druridge Bay looking north: dunes and marram grass for mile after mile:.

Dolerite outcrops in sills and dykes in several places along the Northumberland coast. It is a hard, black, volcanic rock, known locally as whinstone.

Whinstone weathers slowly, revealing criss–cross fissures which wear away to provide some shelter for marine life like limpets. Not many other shellfish can take a firm enough grip to survive for long on the North East shoreline.

Whinstone boulders on the north shore of Holy Island.

A fulmar prospecting for a nest site at Cullernose Point in February. The cliff face shows how dolerite cooled quicky into rough hexagonal columns. The dolerite was 'extruded' into existing sandstone nearly 300 million years ago.

Whinstone ridges called 'heughs' occur like islands in the farmland just behind the coast.
Their slopes are often covered by gorse or scrub trees.

Lichen-covered whinstone dipping into the sea on an exposed section of coast north of Craster.

A shallow rock pool with emerald-green limpets. The colour comes from algae.
Further down the shore, the rock pools are deeper and are under water for longer
between tides – so they provide a better home for crabs, sea urchins and sea anemones.

Scurvy grass flowers in early summer all along the coast. In days of long sea voyages, it was used as a source of vitamin C and is often common around old harbours.

Embleton in May. Cowslips grow on dunes as well as in old meadows.

Craster was a busy little fishing village and a few traditional 'cobles' still use its harbour,
though they no longer catch herrings. Kippers are smoked in Craster and they are delicious.

Craster harbour was built in 1906 to serve a local whin quarry as well as a fishing fleet.
It must have been a noisy, dusty and smelly place – and not very picturesque.

The low cliffs of the far north coast, near Scremerston, are composed
of buckled sediments: layers of limestone, sandstone and shale.

Big whin boulders on the rocky shore at Longhoughton. Barnacles and limpets
are scattered all over the surfaces except on the top south-facing sides, which get
too dry and hot in the summer. Barnacles cannot move to get out of the way,
and limpets like to stay in their own little niche.

Cullernose Point from Howick. Layers of sandstone create shelves or carrs just offshore. In the distance is Cullernose with its cliff face of dolerite colonised by kittiwakes and fulmars (compare this summer picture with the picture on page 50).

Below the lowest tides are forests of kelp. In winter gales the fronds are often ripped by their 'holdfasts' and washed up on the shore. In late winter and spring Boulmer beach can be piled high with a bank of dead seaweed, mainly kelp and wracks. The seaweed attracts sandhoppers, which are eaten by wading birds like turnstones and redshanks.

The Aln is one of the few Northumberland rivers with a lowland reach and a slow-flowing set of meanders. The water here is tidal and salty, a mile from the muddy estuary at Alnmouth. The village of Lesbury is in the distance, to the west.

Continuing the Aln upstream, looking north-west one morning in late summer.

Early summer in the Aln valley near Lesbury, looking east towards the view on page 45.
The footpath through the barley forks left to Foxton Hall and right to the river bank.

Two miles from
Belford in north
Northumberland –
rich and productive
farmland viewed from
a whinstone heugh.

Harvest time: baling straw next to Budle Bay. It is high tide, so the sea is just visible.

Black-headed and common gulls following a plough. This is two miles from the coast,
so the birds can enjoy the best of both worlds – earthworms and cockles.

The coast path from Howick to Cullernose in early May.

A ploughed field in autumn: Hips Heugh near Howick.

Oilseed rape makes a vibrant and violent impression on the senses – bright enough to give you a headache and make your camera over-compensate. Cresswell Farm near Lynemouth.

Northern marsh orchid –
one of the commonest
flowers in the dune
slacks of Holy Island.

The farm settlement of Beal, about a mile from the Holy Island causeway.

A bright March afternoon, looking east from Easington, over Budle Bay and
Budle Point to the Longstone lighthouse on the Farne Islands.

A big-boned young stirk on the other side of the fence at Cresswell.
In the distance is Cresswell Tower, a medieval stronghold from the Border Wars.

A gipsy horse tethered beside the coast road near Lynemouth.
The skyline – old collieries and power stations – will be transformed over the next few years.

Spring lambs and buttercups.

Border Leicester sheep at their ancestral home of Rock, near Embleton.
The rams are crossed with Cheviot ewes to create half-bred lambs – still a popular breed in the Wooler area.

Breakfast hay at Alnmouth. An icy morning, with frost on the backs of the sheep.

Farm settlements near the coast were created in the eighteenth and nineteenth centuries to accommodate self-contained communities of land labourers.

Jack-by-the-hedge,
or garlic mustard, is
one of the commonest
hedgerow plants
in spring.

An orange tip butterfly on cuckoo flower. The female orange tip (which has no orange on its wings) lays its eggs on either jack-by-the-hedge or cuckoo flower.

Warkworth Parish Church – mainly Norman with some alterations by the Percy family who owned the nearby castle (and much of the county). The churchyard includes some attractive old graves, including the huntsman's tomb of 1630.

The north side of Warkworth churchyard, on a twist of the River Coquet.

Apart from the Tyne
and the Tweed, very few
Northumberland rivers are
very deep or dangerous.
This ford across the Aln
is usually only a few
inches deep, just right
for a determined cyclist.

Lesbury Church near Alnmouth.

Burnet rose: white petals, very sharp thorns, and the
most wonderful scent of any wild flower.

The River Coquet in
September. Willowherb
and butterbur line
the banks.

In medieval times, Berwick-upon-Tweed was one of the most affluent towns in Britain, which is why it
was so frequently fought over in the Border Wars. Berwick is now best-known for its bridges,
its Elizabethan town walls and a football team which plays in the Scottish league.

The north side of the Tweed at Berwick, looking over Meadow Haven to the beacon of Sandstell Point.

The Old Castle Walls,
along the riverside path
at Berwick.

Autumn in the grounds of
Howick Hall. Deciduous
woodland is scarce in
Northumberland, but
there are some very pretty
nooks and crannies along
denes and stream-sides
close to the coast.

Spring woodland at
Howick Hall, with drifts
of wood forget-me-not.

Bamburgh village green at Easter. The village is dwarfed by the great castle, extensively rebuilt at the turn of the twentieth century.

Immense and immutable: Bamburgh Castle stands on a whinstone promontory and dominates coast views for twenty miles.

Ida, first King of
Northumbria, built a
fortification at Bamburgh
in 547, but this was pillaged
by the Danes and had to
be rebuilt several times. A
much grander castle was
built in Norman times and
it became a major strategic
stronghold. Bamburgh's
eventual demise was the
result of an artillery
bombardment in the
Wars of the Roses.

Black Rock and Budle Point, looking north-west across Budle Bay and Ross Back Sands to Holy Island and Lindisfarne Castle.

Lindisfarne Castle – a pocket-sized, sixteenth-century structure on top of a dolerite dyke called Beblowe
Hill. The castle was built to guard Holy Island's harbour but never saw much action and was only
garrisoned by a handful of soldiers. Most deaths here were the result of epidemics rather than warfare.

Lindisfarne Castle and the harbour or Ouse at full tide.

Lindisfarne Castle framed by a gap in a ruined wall on The Heugh.

Dunstanburgh Castle,
looking out from the
Keep to Lilburn Tower.
The ruins are haunted
by the ghost of Sir Guy
the Seeker.

Not very much is left of Dunstanburgh but its skeletal remains are impressive. The castle was built in the fourteenth century by Thomas, second Earl of Lancaster. After his execution in 1322 it became the stronghold of John of Gaunt.

The town of Warkworth lies in a twist of the River Coquet. The castle dates back to the twelfth century
but was altered and extended through the Middle Ages. In its heyday it was the residence of the
Earls of Northumberland and was the setting for part of Shakespeare's *Henry IV*.

Warkworth Castle: the keep from the thirteenth-century gatehouse.

The ruins of Warkworth Castle have been teetering on the brink of the Coquet for centuries.
English Heritage tries to ensure that nothing more drops off.

Warkworth's honey-
coloured stonework has
grown old gracefully.

The Aln estuary, viewed
through the window of a
ruined nineteenth-century
chapel on Church Hill.

Dunstanburgh Castle and Gull Crag from the north. An unusually low tide has revealed a kelp bed close to Saddle Rock.

Across Embleton Bay from Newton Point.

Holy Island gained its name and fame from its monastery and saints, and from the Lindisfarne Bible which was created here. Nothing remains of the original monastery or church, which would have been built of wood. Everything was destroyed by Viking raids, and the monks left in 875 taking their relics with them.

Holy Island Priory was built in 1093 and it makes a picturesque ruin. Lindisfarne Castle is in the far distance.

Waste not want not: half an upturned boat makes a very passable workshed.
Holy Island, next to the harbour.

Pieces of a shipwreck, on the boulder shore of Holy Island's north coast.

Drystone wall, Holy Island.

Fulmars on the
lichen-covered face
of Beblowe Hill,
Holy Island.

Digging for bait on the shore near Marden Rocks, south of Boulmer.

Emanuel Point at the
north-east tip of Holy
Island. The huge stone
beacon, painted white,
is visible from miles
out to sea.

The only way to reach Ross Back Sands is to park at Ross and walk across the links.
The sweep of exposed sand stretches for three miles and is nearly always deserted.

Lobster pots and fishing boats at Boulmer.

Silver and gold sunrise: the North Sea in February.

The mouth of the Aln. The outfall has changed over the years: it used to meet the sea south of Church Hill.

Gorse in flower on The Heugh, north of Craster, with Dunstanburgh on the skyline.

Dense spiny gorse bushes make safe nesting sites for several birds such as linnets and yellowhammers.
In some places old rabbit burrows hidden beneath gorse banks are used by shelducks.
Gorse flowers have a heavy coconut scent, which attracts hive bees in the spring.

Eider ducks and a coble in Seahouses harbour.

Seahouses used to make its living from fishing but these days it relies on tourism. Boat trips to the Farne Islands are booked beside the pier. Inner Farne, largest and nearest of the Farne group, is on the skyline to the left of the kiosk.

Seahouses harbour at low tide.

Rain over the Farne Islands at dawn. The view is from Bamburgh, with Longstone at the far left and Inner Farne to the right.

The Farne Islands from Brock Burn at Monks House.

The two best bird islands to visit are Staple and Inner Farne. Staple Island supports large numbers of kittiwake, shag and guillemot.

The needles or stacks off Staple Island are famous for their seabirds: guillemots
nest on the top, with razorbills and kittiwakes on ledges and clefts.

Puffins nest in burrows, so they are found on Inner Farne where there is a covering of turf.

The Arctic tern is an elegant and fragile-looking bird but each year it flies to the sub-Antarctic and back. On Inner Farne, it creates havoc among visitors by dive-bombing anyone who goes near its nest.

One of the main attractions of the Farne Islands is how approachable the birds are. A nestful of shags only two or three feet from the path, Staple Island.

A firm mooring at Beadnell harbour, with serrated wrack and a brittle star.

Lobster pots stacked
ready for action,
Beadnell harbour.

Low tide – north across
Budle Bay.

Budle Bay and the meandering channel of Budle Water. On the skyline are the Kyloe Hills.

Incoming tide, Newton Haven.

Pebbles on the beach, Amble Braid.

Saltpan Rocks and Seahouse, from the Scremerston shore south of Berwick.

Alnmouth harbour looking west, upstream to the Aln.

Monks House was once owned by the Lindisfarne monks who launched their boats from here to row out to Inner Farne. This group of buildings was adapted into a bird observatory in the 1950s, managed by the wildlife artist Eric Ennion.

Newton Haven from Newton Point. A popular wind-surfing centre and one of the best areas for wildlife along the coast. There is a nature reserve just inland from Low Newton village.

Farmland and a whinstone heugh. The skyline is broken by the distant tops of Cheviot and Hedgehope.

Thrift flowers in early June.

Sandstone weathers along its bedding planes, creating some bizarre patterns.
Howick Haven, south of the Rumbling Kern.

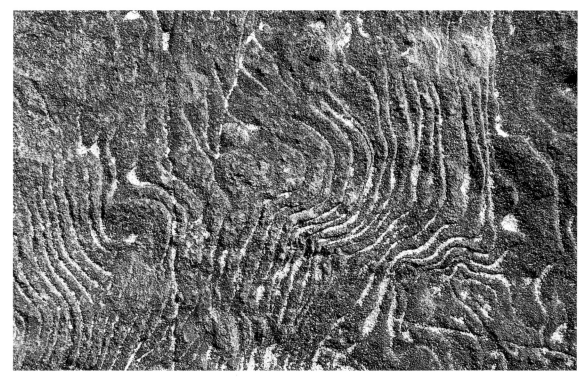

Weathered gritstone with blown sand, Cresswell.

These concrete blocks were meant to deter Hitler's invasion army and they obviously worked. The blocks are very durable and have withstood the tides for over sixty years. Amble Braid, on the north side of the Coquet near Warkworth.

Buckled sediments on
the cliffs at Howick.

North towards Birling
Carrs. Alnmouth is
hidden in an early
morning mist or 'fret'.

Rain approaching Holy Island from the Cheviots. The two needles at the north tip of Ross Back Sands were built to guide in the Holy Island fishing fleet.

Heavy mist with a disappearing sun, Howick.

A giant wind turbine
off the coast at Blythe.
Passing boats look like toys.

Low Hauxley, a few yards from the sea.

A lock-up on Holy Island, between the harbour and the priory.

Silver...

...and gold.

Sailing boats high and
dry, Alnmouth harbour.

Near Skerrs, north of Cheswick: beds of sandstone and limestone sloping into the sea.

Sunshine and showers. Marram and lyme grass on the dunes of Budle Point.

Church Hill across the Aln estuary.
The hill was much bigger before the river changed course and was the site of a Norman church.

The Holy Island causeway at dawn, from the mainland (Beal) side. The tide has just ebbed from the road and for the next seven or eight hours it will be safe to drive on and off the island. The posts to the right mark the old pilgrims' route over the sands.

Sunrise from the Holy Island side of Beal Sands. A common seal is hauled out on the shore.

Misty sunrise, Druridge Bay.